Step - by - Step
COCKTAILS

Step - by - Step
COCKTAILS

JENNY RIDGWELL

PHOTOGRAPHED BY
JON STEWART

GREENWICH EDITIONS

Published 1999 by Greenwich Editions,
10 Blenheim Court, Brewery Road, London N7 9NT

A member of the Chrysalis Group plc
©Merehurst Limited 1986

ISBN 0 862 88 2761

Editor: Chris Fayers
Designers: Roger Daniels, Richard Slater, Stuart Willard
Photographer: Jon Stewart
Drinks mixed by Chris Isaacs and Vernon Lee
Typeset by Lineage
Colour separation by New Interlitho S.p.A., Milan
Printed and bound in Spain by Just Colour Graphic, S.L.

ACKNOWLEDGEMENTS
The publishers would like to thank the following for their help and advice:

Brian Page: President of United Kingdom Bartenders Guild
Citrus Marketing Board of Israel
Elizabeth David Limited, 46 Bourne Street, London SW1
and at Covent Garden Kitchen Supplies, 3 North Row, The Market, London WC2
Garden Store, 26 Procter Street, London WC1V 6NX
Hiram Walker International
Joey Bussey and David Barrett
Specialist garnishing tools "Kustom Kutters" - supplied by M. Gilbert (Greenford) Ltd
Noel's Cocktail Accessories
Peppermint Park, 13/14 Upper Saint Martins Lane, London WC2
Philips Home Appliances, City House, 420-430 London Road, Croydon, CR9 3QR
The Covent Garden General Store, 111 Long Acre, Covent Garden, London WC2E 9NT and The Piccadilly Circus General Store,
20 Shaftesbury Avenue, Piccadilly, London W1V 7DB
The General Trading Company, 144 Sloane Street, Sloane Square, London SW1X 9BL
The Glass Department, Harrods Limited, Knightsbridge, London SW1
The Ritz Bartenders

CONTENTS

INTRODUCTION 7

EQUIPMENT 8

GLASSES 9

GARNISHES 10

FROSTINGS 17

FLAVOURFUL TOPPINGS 18

ICE 19

ACCOMPANIMENTS 20

GIN BASED DRINKS 23

WHISKY BASED DRINKS 29

VODKA BASED DRINKS 33

RUM BASED DRINKS 39

BRANDY BASED DRINKS 43

WINE BASED DRINKS 46

CHAMPAGNE BASED DRINKS 48

OTHER MIXED DRINKS 50

NON-ALCOHOL BASED DRINKS 58

GLOSSARY 63

INDEX 64

INTRODUCTION

WHAT IS A COCKTAIL?

The modern definition of a cocktail is a drink composed of at least two ingredients which have been shaken or stirred together, and served either as a tall or short drink.

Mixed drinks have been prepared for centuries, but the first mention of the cocktail in print appeared in the New York periodical, Balance, dated May 13th 1806. It read, "A Cocktail is a stimulating liqueur, composed of spirits of any kind, sugar, water and bitters - it is vulgarly called bittered sling and supposed to be an electioneering potion".

The United States made cocktail drinking popular, especially during the 1920s when many of today's famous cocktails were invented. Over the last few years there has been a growing interest in cocktails. New drinks and mixers, often made from exotic ingredients, have been introduced from all over the world and delicious, colourful new recipes have been developed.

MEASURES

For this book, the quantities of liquid ingredients are specified in "measures" (msrs.) or parts of a measure. A standard measure is one-sixth of a gill, which is slightly less than one fluid ounce or twenty-five to thirty millilitres. A "dash" is simply the quantity released in a quick spurt from a bottle. To start with, measure drinks accurately in order to achieve each recipe. Later, recipes can be adapted to suit your own taste. Some of the recipes are given in metric/cup/imperial measurements, where quantities are too large to be measured as above. Use one set of measurements only as they are not exact equivalents.

HINTS AND TIPS FOR COCKTAIL MAKING

● Keep equipment and work surfaces clean - a dirty glass with poor garnish does not look attractive.

● Use good quality ingredients - the flavour of most cocktails is delicate and poor products can spoil the taste. Fruit used for garnish should always be of the best quality.

● Handle glasses by the stem or base to avoid smears.

● Most cocktails should be served in chilled glasses.

● Plan ahead when preparing special drinks. Have a good supply of ice, beaten egg whites, sugar syrup, freshly squeezed lemon juice and seasoned tomato juice if they are to be used.

● The size and colour of the garnish should complement the style of the drink and the size and type of the glass used.

● Prepare slices of fruit for garnish in advance and keep, covered with plastic wrap, in the refrigerator.

● It is usual to stir clear drinks and shake or blend drinks which contain fruit juices, egg white or cream.

● Never fill a glass to the brim, as this makes drinking difficult and the drink may spill.

● Carbonated liquids are usually added last to maintain maximum fizz.

● Serve cocktails as soon as they are mixed. The drink could separate or become diluted by the ice.

Be thoughtful of friends' personal preference and safety and always provide interesting non-alcoholic drinks for them.

THE STORE CUPBOARD

To make an interesting range of cocktails it is useful to keep a basic store cupboard. Whilst there is no need to spend a large amount, investment in bottled stock might include the following: bourbon, cherry brandy, Cognac, Cointreau, crème de cassis, crème de menthe, Curaçao, Galliano, gin, Grenadine, Kahlua, Malibu, melon liqueur, rum - light and dark, Tequila, vermouth - dry and sweet, vodka and whisky. Small bottles of other spirits and liqueurs can be bought as required.

Keep a range of mixers and seasonings handy to be able to make a variety of drinks. Mixers for tall drinks can be kept chilled in the refrigerator. The following ingredients are basic: coconut cream, grapefruit, orange, pineapple and tomato juice, tropical fruit juices, lemonade, mineral water, soda and tonic waters.

Keep a selection of ingredients ready for garnishing or flavouring drinks: olives, cherries, canned consommé, salt, celery salt, grated nutmeg, ground cinnamon and cinnamon sticks, oranges, lemons, limes, cucumber, celery, mint, Tabasco and Worcestershire sauces, Angostura bitters, orange flower water.

EQUIPMENT

The right equipment makes preparing cocktails easy.

Cocktail Shaker: professional bartenders usually prefer a shaker consisting of two cones, which overlap when fitted together. The drink is then poured using a separate strainer.

For beginners, a three piece shaker consisting of a base, top with built in strainer and a fitted cap is adequate. When no shaker is available, improvise using a screwtop jar with a wide rim.

To use a shaker, add the ice and cocktail ingredients, secure the parts together and, holding the shaker with both hands, shake briskly. When the shaker becomes frosty on the outside, the cocktail is sufficiently chilled and should be served immediately to avoid dilution by melting ice.

Strainer: used when pouring drinks from shaker to glass, so that ice and fruit are held back. The best strainers are made from stainless steel and look like a flat spoon with holes in.

Mixing glass: used for mixing tall drinks, it is similar to a jug without a handle and has a pouring lip.

Blender: used for aerating cocktails.

Other useful equipment: long handled spoon, teaspoon, tablespoon, measure, ice bucket and tongs, corkscrew, bottle opener, chopping board, paring knife, lemon squeezer, cloth, cocktail sticks, straws, stirrers and ice crusher, such as a wooden mallet or rolling pin. A vegetable peeler or canelle knife, which has a handle and flat circle of metal with a sharp lip on one side, is useful for preparing decorated fruit and vegetable garnishes.

GLASSES

With so many different shapes, sizes and colours in glassware, choosing a suitable glass for a certain drink requires thought. There are classic shapes which suit some cocktails, but nowadays the traditional choice of glass is not that important.

Champagne drinks look attractive when served in a champagne flute and short cocktails may be served in Martini glasses.

Taller drinks need larger glasses and here the choice is more difficult. For tall drinks with little or no garnish, such as a Bloody Mary or Hummer, a tall highball glass is suitable. Some exotic drinks which are lavishly garnished with slices of fruit, straws and other decorations need to be served in a substantial glass such as a large goblet. If smaller glasses with narrow necks are heavily garnished, the decoration will interfere with drinking and the effect will not be pleasing.

There are many intriguing glasses available, but beware of overdoing things! Coloured glass can spoil the effect of a drink — a dark glass will detract from a delicately pale drink such as a Pink Lady. Heavily patterned glasses can be used, but be sparing with the decoration or the finished result will appear cluttered.

Most important of all, use spotlessly clean glasses. Wash and rinse the glasses in hot water, dry them while still warm and polish with a clean, soft cloth. Check glasses before using and repolish them if necessary.

TYPES OF GLASSES AVAILABLE

Cocktail or Martini glass: a tall, wide rimmed glass with a tall stem, used for Pink Lady and, of course, Martini.

Brandy balloon: this glass is designed to trap the fragrance of the brandy in the bowl of the glass, so both the aroma and the flavour can be enjoyed.

Wine glass: there are many types of wine glasses so choose a style that is pleasant to drink from. White and red wines can be served in the same style of glass, although traditionally white wine glasses are smaller and have a longer stem.

Liqueur glass: a small glass for serving small measures.

Highball or Tall glass: a tall, usually straight sided glass holding about 315ml (1¼ cups/10 fluid oz.). Tall drinks mixed with fruit juices or lemonade are best served in highball glasses.

Large goblet: these glasses vary in size and shape. They are used for serving tall mixed drinks with plenty of ice. Exotic drinks, such as Mai Tai or Tropical Cocktail, are best served in goblets. The wide rims allow scope for imaginative decoration without looking cluttered.

Champagne glass: a tall fluted glass with a tall stem used for Champagne cocktails and Ritz Fizz.

Old fashioned or whisky tumbler: a short tumbler with straight or sloping sides which usually holds about 125ml (½cup/4 fluid oz.). Suitable for plain fruit juices, Rusty Nail and of course, Old Fashioned.

Tulip glass: a tall, tulip shaped glass, often used for champagne drinks.

CITRUS GARNISHES

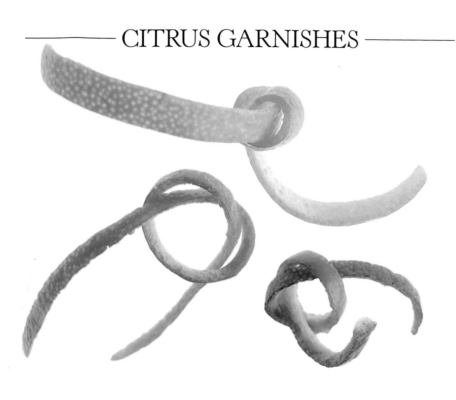

Choose firm, good coloured fruit with unblemished skin. Wash the fruit just before use. A spiral of peel can be used to decorate tall drinks. Pare off about a 2-3 inch strip of peel in a continuous spiral using a canelle knife or vegetable peeler. Take care not to cut into bitter white pith.

Use spiral to hang over rim of the glass into drink.

A knot of peel can be used to add zest to some drinks. Remove strips of peel using a canelle knife or vegetable peeler. Tie each strip into a knot. This releases the fragrant oils from peel. Drop into drink immediately.

A plain slice can be used to decorate drinks. Place orange, lemon or lime on its side and cut crosswise segments with a sharp stainless steel knife, (a carbon steel knife will discolour flesh).

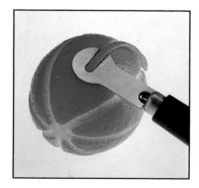

A decorated slice can be used to garnish a simple drink. Peel may be decorated by scoring skin with a canelle knife or vegetable peeler. Pull knife round orange, lemon or lime from top to bottom to expose pith. Repeat to make eight divisions.

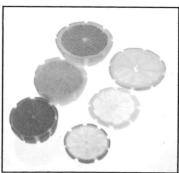

Place orange, lemon or lime on its side and cut into thin slices.

CITRUS GARNISHES

Plain and decorated slices can be used in different ways to garnish drinks. Cut through to centre of whole or half slice and place slice on edge of glass. Here, a blood orange is used to give an attractive effect.

Using a cocktail stick, double up whole slice with cherry in middle. Twist whole or half slices using cocktail stick and balance across rim of glass. A pineapple leaf can be added, if desired.

Twist slices from different coloured citrus fruits together.

Cut shapes from fruit peel using a sharp knife or cutter. Float on top of drinks, such as Mulled Wine.

Special cutters can be used to create unusual designs.

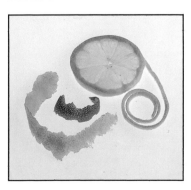

A strip of peel can be used to add zest to drinks, such as Martini or Manhattan. Remove thin short strips of zest using a sharp stainless steel knife. Longer strips of peel may be used for larger drinks, adding more flavour.

FRUIT GARNISHES

Strawberry
Choose firm, ripe strawberries with good, green-leaved tops to garnish strawberry flavoured drinks and white wine punches.
Cut strawberry in half lengthwise using a stainless steel knife to prevent discolouration. Use in white wine punches.

Replace green-leaved top of strawberry with sprig of fresh mint.

Make about a 2.5cm (1in) cut into whole strawberry from tip to top, and balance on the glass rim. Cut several times to make a fan.

Kumquat
Kumquats are eaten whole with the peel on. Cut 4 or more sections in the peel with a sharp knife and gently pull each section open to create a kumquat flower. The fruit may also be speared on to a cocktail stick with other fruits, such as pineapple and cherries.

Kiwi Fruit
Kiwi fruit adds interesting colour to a fruit garnish. Wash fruit and use unpeeled. Cut kiwi fruit into crosswise slices. Make a cut to centre of slice and place on edge of glass.

Add segments of kiwi fruit to other fruit for decoration. Cut lengthwise and make an upwards incision.

Banana
Banana may be used to decorate drinks such as Banana Cow and other exotic cocktails. Choose firm, unblemished fruit with good yellow peel and prepare just before serving. Cut unpeeled bananas into slices. Dip in to lemon juice to prevent discolouration.

Make cut into centre of slice and place on rim of glass with a cherry.

FRUIT GARNISHES

Papaya or pawpaw
Tropical fruit juices are popular mixes for tall drinks and papaya makes an interesting garnish. Choose fruit that is firm but gives slightly with a gentle thumb press. The skin should be unblemished and varies from green to yellow; use unpeeled. Cut fruit in half lengthwise and remove black seeds.

Cut slices lengthwise to decorate large goblets, making an incision in flesh to help balance on glass.

Cut across papaya and spear small pieces on to cocktail stick with other fruits, such as a cherry and slice of starfruit.

Form balls using a melon scoop and spear on to cocktail stick. Add pineapple leaves to decorate.

Apple
Choose apples with bright red or green skins. Wash before use. Cut apple segments from unpeeled fruit and use to decorate glass. Dip into lemon juice to prevent discolouration.

Cut whole apple in to crosswise slices and float in fruit or wine punches.

Starfruit
Choose unblemished yellow or green fruit and wash before use. Cut across fruit to make star shaped slices and either balance on glass rim or float in drink.

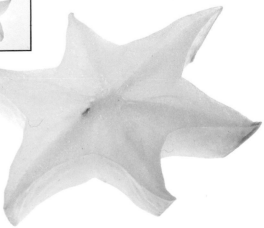

FRUIT GARNISHES

Melon

Melons make an interesting garnish for green or yellow coloured drinks, especially those using a melon liqueur. Cut slices of watermelon from a small melon with dark green skin. Make incision in flesh to help balance slice on glass. Add a cherry to decorate.

Use a melon scoop to remove balls from different types of melon for a colourful presentation.

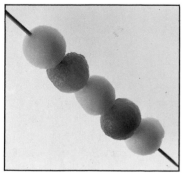

Spear melon balls on cocktail stick and serve with short drinks.

COCONUT GARNISHES

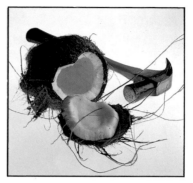

To open coconut, pierce "eyes" of coconut with a sharp implement and hammer and drain out coconut water. Tap coconut with hammer to crack shell and scoop out flesh with a blunt knife. Alternatively, place coconut in a preheated 180C (350F/Gas 4) oven for about 10 minutes, then transfer to a board and use hammer to split shell. The flesh will have shrunk away from the skin, allowing easier removal. If whole coconut is used for serving, cut off top with a saw.

Drape 4 coconut segments over edge of glass for exotic drinks. Cut ½cm (¼in) thick segments from the nut, using a sharp knife and make incision in flesh to help balance coconut on edge of glass. Frost glass with dried coconut mixed with green colouring and add 2 green cherries speared on a cocktail stick.

Use coconut curls to decorate rim of glass. Level edge of coconut with a knife. Pare off thin peelings of coconut, including brown skin, with a very sharp knife, so that they curl up.

Grate coconut flesh on a coarse grater, including brown skin and sprinkle on top of drinks.

PINEAPPLE GARNISHES

To use the whole pineapple for serving, carefully cut off the top with its spiny leaves, about 5cm (2in) below the leaf growth.

Scoop out the centre of the pineapple using a sharp knife and spoon. The flesh may be blended for fresh pineapple juice or used for fruit salad.

Fill the pineapple with the prepared drink, replace top and serve with suitable garnish and straw.

Pineapple leaves can be used as a garnish with other fruits. Remove the best spiny leaves by easing them out gently from the head.

Pineapple slices are used to decorate very large drinks and fruit punches. The pineapple is sweetest at the top, near the spiny leaves, so these slices taste best. Lay the pineapple on its side and cut slices approximately 1.5-2cm (½-¾in) thick using a stainless steel knife. Leave on the outside rind as this gives colour and texture to the garnish. Cut the slice through to the centre, garnish with a cherry and 3 pineapple leaves and place on edge of glass.

Half slices may be used to garnish cocktails with a tropical flavour. Cut slice in half, make an incision through to centre and place on edge of glass. Decorate with 3 pineapple leaves and a cherry.

PINEAPPLE GARNISHES

Quarter slices make an attractive decoration for small glasses. Cut halfway to centre and place on edge of glass. Decorate with 2 pineapple leaves and a cherry.

Lengthwise slices can be used to decorate long tall glasses. Cut a small pineapple in half lengthwise. Cut off a segment and make an incision parallel with the pineapple core. Place on the outside edge of the glass. The top of the pineapple may be left on the segment.

Pineapple pieces can be used to decorate short drinks. Divide a slice of pineapple into 8 equal pieces by cutting diametrically 4 times.

Spear the pieces with a cocktail stick and use for a garnish with coloured cherries and pineapple leaves.

CHERRIES & FLOWERS

Cherries
There are many kinds of cocktail cherries available. In addition to the traditional red or green, cherries are coloured yellow, blue, purple and orange and may be flavoured with an appropriate liqueur. Spear cherries with a cocktail stick or float on a drink. Choose a colour to complement the recipe.

Serve pitted cherries on edge of drink or speared on cocktail stick. A pair of cherries is particularly attractive. Use fresh or cocktail cherries for decoration.

Roses
Rose petals and buds can be used to decorate drinks, such as Ritz Fizz. Choose a tiny, perfect petal or bud and balance it on top of drink.

Orchids
Delicate orchids are available in sprays from florists. For a special occasion, spear 2 orchids on a cocktail stick and balance on edge of glass. Select the orchid colour to complement the drink.

CUCUMBER GARNISHES

Cucumber strips can be used to decorate tall, clear drinks, such as Pimms. Choose a straight, dark green cucumber and wash and dry before use. Use a canelle knife or vegetable peeler to score along the green skin of the cucumber. Pull the canelle knife towards you, taking off strips of peel.

Cucumber twirls can be hung over the edge of a glass. Peel in a circular movement around the cucumber to produce a twirl.

Decorated cucumber slices can be used to float in clear drinks, or cut to centre and balanced on the edge of a glass. Score along length of cucumber with a canelle knife or vegetable peeler, removing 10 to 14 strips of peel. Using a vegetable knife, cut the cucumber into slices.

Cucumber sticks make a tasty stirrer for savoury drinks, especially those using tomato juice. Cut off the ends of the cucumber. Cut the cucumber in half lengthwise, then slice each half into sticks.

FROSTINGS

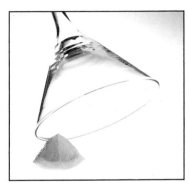

Salt
Margarita or Salty Dog can be served in a salt-frosted glass. Hold the glass upside down by its stem to prevent the juice from running down the bowl of the glass and wipe the outside of the glass with a wedge of lemon.

Dip the glass into a dish of salt, until the rim is evenly coated. Celery salt makes an interesting frosting for drinks such as Bloody Mary.

Sugar
The glass may be wiped with lemon juice or, for a sweeter frosting, dip the glass in lightly beaten egg white.

Dip the glass into a bowl of sugar. Caster sugar may be used or, for the more adventurous, try coloured or natural brown sugars. Alternatively the glass may be dipped in Grenadine or food colouring and then into a bowl of caster sugar to give a coloured frosting.

FROSTINGS

Coconut

For coconut based drinks, dip the glass into beaten egg white and then into a bowl of dried coconut. Coconut can be tossed with food colouring for a coloured frosting. Here, the dried coconut has been mixed with a little blue food colouring.

Coffee and Chocolate

For coffee and chocolate liqueur based drinks, wipe glass with lemon juice or egg white. Dip into instant coffee powder, finely ground coffee beans or cocoa mixed with a little caster sugar.

FLAVOURFUL TOPPINGS

Nutmeg

Creamy or milky drinks are delicious with a sprinkling of nutmeg. Grate a little of the whole nutmeg on to a plate using a fine grater. Sprinkle carefully on to drink. (Grating directly on to the drink may spoil the finished presentation.) Always grate nutmeg just before serving to prevent loss of flavour.

Cinnamon

Whole sticks of cinnamon may be served with Mulled Wine or Egg Nog to give flavour and to act as a stirrer. Freshly ground cinnamon can be made by grinding the sticks in a coffee grinder. Sprinkle carefully on to drink.

Coffee

A sprinkling of instant coffee powder may be used on top of coffee flavoured drinks. Alternatively, fresh coffee beans may be finely ground in a coffee or spice grinder.

Chocolate

Chocolate may be grated using a fine or coarse grater and sprinkled over drinks. Chocolate sticks make an interesting garnish for thick, sweet drinks. Twirls of chocolate can be used on top of ice cream and whipped cream. Pull the blade of a sharp knife or vegetable peeler along a block of slightly warm chocolate. The chocolate will curl as it is worked.

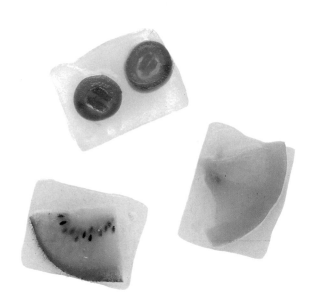

ICE

Ice cubes are usually made in oblong ice trays, but experiment with fancy shaped moulds for fun. If tap water produces cloudy ice, try using still, spring or distilled water. For large parties, make up a quantity of ice cubes in advance or buy commercially made ice.

Cracked ice is used in cocktail shakers and chills the drink quickly. Wrap the ice cubes in a clean tea towel and place on a firm surface. Hit the ice with a wooden mallet or rolling pin until the ice has broken into small pieces.

Crushed ice is broken more finely than cracked ice. Ice can be prepared in advance and kept in a plastic bag in the freezing compartment.

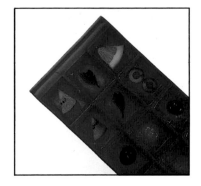

Decorated ice cubes can be used in clear drinks. Fill the ice cube tray half full of water and freeze. Dip decoration, such as mint leaves, cherries, slices of orange or lemon segments, kiwi fruit, small kumquats, red currants or slices of stuffed olive in water. Place on the ice cube and freeze until firm.

Top up the ice cubes with cold water and freeze.

Coloured and flavoured ice cubes can be used to complement the choice of drink. Make ice cubes from cold coffee, tea, ginger ale, fruit juices, such as orange and apple. One half of the cube may be a different colour – simply freeze one layer, such as blackcurrant juice, then freeze the other layer, such as water. Cubes may be flavoured, for example, Angostura bitters to use in Pink Gin.

Frozen Lemon Slices can be used in drinks in place of fresh lemon. Cut lemon into slices and place on a tray in the freezing compartment. Once frozen, lift off, place in a freezer bag, label and tie up.

Serve cocktails in chilled glasses. Place glass in freezer until frosted or swirl an ice cube around the glass for a few minutes to achieve the same effect. Do not place very fragile glasses in freezer, as they may crack in the extreme temperature. Remove ice cubes before adding drink.

ACCOMPANIMENTS

Plantain Chips

1-2 large green plantains
oil for deep frying
salt, black pepper, paprika

Cut off both ends of the plantain, peel and cut into thin slices, about 1cm (½in) thick.

Deep fry in hot oil for 2-4 minutes until golden brown and crisp.

Drain on absorbent paper towels and sprinkle with salt, black pepper and paprika.

Avocado Dip

2 very ripe avocados
juice of ½ lemon or lime
dash of hot pepper sauce or Tabasco sauce
salt and black pepper
paprika

Scoop out the flesh from the avocados.

Blend all the ingredients together in a processor or mash together with a fork. Serve in a small dish, garnished with a sprinkling of paprika.

Hot Spicy Sauce

2 tablespoons tomato paste
juice of ½ lemon
hot pepper sauce or Tabasco sauce
fresh herbs, such as basil or parsley, finely chopped

Mix together the tomato paste, lemon juice and pepper sauce to taste. Serve in a small dish as a dip, garnished with a sprinkling of finely chopped herbs.

In the Caribbean, plantain chips are often served instead of crisps. They make an unusual nibble served with avocado dip and a hot spicy sauce.

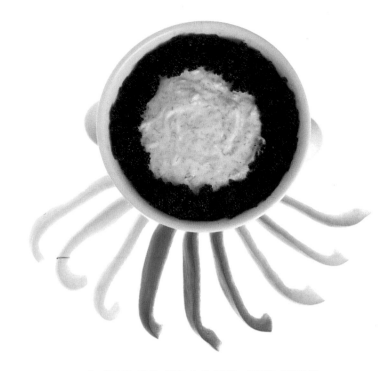

Peppers with creamy cucumber dip

1 each red, green, yellow pepper (capsicum), to serve
½ cucumber
250g (1 cup/8oz.) cream cheese
1 clove garlic, crushed
1 tablespoon mayonnaise
2 teaspoons finely chopped dill,
salt to taste
milk
caviar or lump fish roe
paprika

Wash the peppers, cut off the tops and discard. Cut the peppers in half lengthwise and remove the white pith and seeds. Cut into long strips 1cm (½in) wide. Set aside.
Grate the unpeeled cucumber on a fine grater or purée in a processor.

In a medium bowl, beat together the cream cheese, garlic, mayonnaise, dill and salt with enough milk to make a smooth dip.
Stir in the cucumber. Transfer the dip to a serving dish. Spoon a little caviar or lump fish roe around the edge of the dish and sprinkle with paprika. Place the dish in the centre of a round plate or tray and surround with pepper slices.

Cheesy puffs

30g (2 tablespoons/1 oz.) butter
155ml (⅔ cup/5 fluid oz.) water
75g (½ cup/2½ oz.) flour
90g (⅔ cup/3 oz.) strong flavoured grated cheese
2 teaspoons grated Parmesan cheese
pinch paprika
pinch mustard powder
1 egg
Toppings: mustard seeds, caraway seeds, fennel seeds, sesame seeds, paprika, grated Parmesan.

In a small saucepan, boil together the butter and water until the butter melts. Remove from heat and stir in the flour, cheeses, paprika and mustard. Return to the heat and cook an additional 2-3 minutes, beating constantly with a wooden spoon to form a paste which comes away from the sides of the pan. Remove from the heat.
In a small bowl, whisk the egg. Slowly stir into the mixture and beat until thoroughly combined.
Preheat the oven to 200C (400F/Gas 6). Lightly grease baking sheets. Place a 1cm (½in) plain nozzle into a large pastry bag and fill the bag with the mixture. Pipe 20-25 small mounds of mixture on to baking sheet. Sprinkle with a selection of different toppings. Bake for 15-20 minutes until the puffs are crisp and golden. Serve hot or cold.

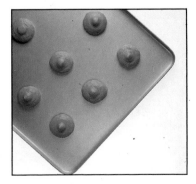

ACCOMPANIMENTS

Spicy Nuts

2 tablespoons oil
2 teaspoons ground cumin
1 teaspoon ground coriander
1 teaspoon paprika
250g (1½ cups/8oz.) mixed nuts, such as
brazils, cashews, hazelnuts, almonds, pecans,
peanuts
salt to taste

Anchovy Toasties

8-10 anchovy fillets
60g (¼ cup/2oz.) butter
½ teaspoon lemon juice
6 slices brown bread, crusts removed
stuffed olives, sliced

Preheat oven to 190C (375F/Gas 5).
Chop the anchovy fillets finely.

Preheat oven to 180C (350F/Gas 4).
Heat the oil in a large saucepan. Add the
spices and cook for 2-3 minutes. Stir in
the nuts and toss well for 5 minutes.
Season with salt.

Beat them together with the butter and
lemon juice to form a smooth paste.

Transfer the mixture to a baking sheet
and bake for 15 minutes. Cool before
serving. The nuts may be stored in a
glass jar for several weeks.

Toast the bread on one side. Spread
evenly with the anchovy paste. Place on
a baking sheet and bake for 5 minutes
or until the paste begins to bubble. Cut
each slice into 4 triangles or squares.
Serve hot, garnished with a slice of
stuffed olive.

— PINK LADY —

2 msrs. gin

4 dashes Grenadine

1 dash egg white

Shake egg white with Grenadine and
gin. Strain into chilled cocktail glass.

— WHITE LADY —

1 msrs. gin

½ msrs. Cointreau

juice of ½ lemon

1 dash of egg white

Shake together gin, Cointreau and
lemon juice with egg white. Pour into
chilled cocktail glass.

— MARTINI (dry) —

ice cubes

2½ msrs. dry gin

½ msr. dry vermouth

olive and knot of lemon peel

Fill Martini pitcher with ice. Gently
pour in gin. Add vermouth and stir
gently. Strain into chilled Martini glass
and add olive and knot of lemon peel.

— MARTINI (sweet) —

2 msrs. gin

1 msr. sweet vermouth

1 maraschino cherry

Mix gin and vermouth as for dry
Martini (see preceding recipe). Strain
into chilled Martini glass and add
cherry.

— PINK GIN —

3 dashes Angostura bitters

ice cubes

1½ msrs. gin

1 msr. water

Shake bitters into tumbler and rotate to
coat glass. Discard excess. Put ice cubes
in tumbler. Add gin and water and
serve.

— SILVER STREAK —

1½ msrs. gin

1 msr. Kummel

ice cubes

Pour gin and Kummel over ice cubes in
a tumbler and stir.

— ROLES ROYCE —

cracked ice

1 msr. gin

½ msr. dry vermouth

½ msr. sweet vermouth

¼ msr. Benedictine

Stir ice with gin, vermouths and
Benedictine. Strain into Martini glass.

— NEGRONI —

ice cubes

1 msr. dry gin

¾ msr. sweet vermouth

½ msr. Campari bitters

soda water

knot of lemon peel

Stir ice with gin, vermouth and bitters
in mixing glass. Pour into Martini glass,
add splash of soda water and knot of
lemon peel.

— STRAWBERRY DAWN —

1 msr. gin
—
1 msr. coconut cream
—
3 strawberries
—
crushed ice

Mix gin, coconut cream, 2 strawberries
and plenty of crushed ice in a blender.
Pour into a cocktail glass, decorate with
remaining strawberry. Cut into a fan
and serve with short straws.

— RAMOZ FIZZ —

lemon wedge
—
caster sugar
—
cracked ice
—
2 msrs. dry gin
—
1 msr. fresh lemon juice
—
1 msr. fresh lime juice
—
1 msr. whipping cream
—
2 dashes orange flower water
—
1 teaspoon sugar
—
1 egg white
—
soda water
—
1 orchid, if desired

Frost the rim of highball glass with
lemon and sugar. Shake cracked ice with
remaining ingredients except soda
water. Strain into glass, top with soda
water and stir gently. Garnish with an
orchid, if desired.

— BRONX COCKTAIL —

cracked ice

1 msr. dry gin

½ msr. orange juice

1 dash sweet vermouth

1 dash dry vermouth

slice of orange

Shake ice with gin, orange juice and
vermouth. Serve in cocktail glass
decorated with slice of orange.

— JOHN (OR TOM) COLLINS —

ice cubes

2 msrs. dry gin

2 msrs. lemon juice

1 teaspoon sugar (gomme) syrup

soda water

slice of lemon

1 coloured cherry

Place ample ice in large glass. Add gin,
lemon juice and syrup. Top up with
soda water and stir well. Serve with slice
of lemon, cherry and a straw.

— WHISKY COBBLER —

ice cubes

2 msrs. Scotch whisky

4 dashes Curaçao

4 dashes brandy

sprig of mint

slice of orange

chunk of pineapple

Fill goblet with ice cubes. Stir in Scotch,
Curaçao, and brandy. Decorate with
mint and fruit.

— BOURBON MINT JULEP —

2 msrs. bourbon

5 sprigs mint

4 teaspoons sugar

ice cubes

1 dash dark rum or brandy

slice of lemon

Mix bourbon, 4 sprigs of mint and
sugar in small glass. Pour into glass
filled with ice cubes and stir until
outside of glass becomes frosted. Top
with dash of dark rum or brandy.
Garnish with remaining sprig of mint
and slice of lemon. Serve with straws.

—— MANHATTAN (dry) ——

ice cubes

1½ msrs. Canadian whisky

¾ msr. dry vermouth

1 or 2 dashes Angostura bitters

1 olive

knot of lemon peel

Stir ice with whisky, vermouth and
bitters. Strain into Martini glass. Spear
olive with cocktail pick and balance on
edge of glass. Add knot of lemon peel.

—— MANHATTAN (sweet) ——

ice cubes

1½ msrs. Canadian whisky

¾ msr. sweet vermouth

1 dash Angostura bitters

1 maraschino cherry

knot of lemon peel

Stir ice with whisky, vermouth and
bitters. Strain into Martini glass. Spear
cherry with cocktail pick and balance on
edge of glass. Add knot of lemon peel.

— RUSTY NAIL —

1½ msrs. whisky

1½ msrs. Drambuie

ice cubes

strip of lemon peel

Pour whisky and Drambuie on to ice in
tumbler. Add strip of lemon peel.

— OLD FASHIONED —

2 dashes Angostura bitters

1 cube sugar

ice cubes

1 msr. rye or bourbon

twist of lemon peel

1 maraschino cherry

Muddle bitters with sugar cube in old-
fashioned tumbler until sugar is
dissolved. Add ice cubes and rye or
bourbon. Twist lemon peel over drink to
extract zest, drop it in and garnish with
cherry.

— WHISKY SOUR —

ice cubes

1½ msrs. whisky

1 msr. lemon juice

½ msr. sugar (gomme) syrup

twist of lemon peel

Shake ice with whisky, lemon juice and
syrup. Strain into a tumbler and
decorate with twist of lemon peel.

— ROB ROY —

½ msr. whisky

½ msr. sweet vermouth

1 dash Angostura bitters

ice cubes

1 maraschino cherry or twist of lemon
peel

Stir whisky, vermouth and bitters with
ice in pitcher. Pour into cocktail glass
and add cherry or twist of lemon peel.

— BULLSHOT —

1 cube beef bouillon

2 msrs. hot water

lemon wedge

1½ msrs. vodka

ice cubes

salt and lemon juice to frost glass

knot of lemon peel

Dissolve bouillon cube in hot water.
Add a squeeze of lemon and the vodka
and stir briskly. Pour over ice in tumbler,
frosted with salt and lemon. Add a knot
of lemon peel. (Rum may be substituted
for vodka and celery salt for salt to frost
glass.)

— SURF RIDER —

3 msrs. vodka

1 msr. sweet vermouth

juice of 1 orange

juice of ½ lemon

½ teaspoon Grenadine

cracked ice

3 maraschino cherries

Pour vodka, vermouth, fruit juices and
Grenadine over ice in shaker. Shake
until frosty. Strain into glass. Garnish
with cherries. Serve with straws.

— BIKINI —

3 msrs. vodka

juice of ½ lemon

1 msr. white rum

½ msr. milk

1 teaspoon sugar

cracked ice

Pour vodka, lemon juice, white rum,
milk and sugar over ice in shaker. Shake
until frosty. Strain into glass.

— BLOODSHOT —

cracked ice

1 msr. vodka

2 msrs. condensed consommé

2 msrs. tomato juice

1 dash lemon juice

1 dash Worcestershire sauce

celery salt

2 slices of cucumber

Mix ice with vodka, consommé, tomato
juice, lemon juice and Worcestershire
sauce in shaker. Pour into tall glass.
Sprinkle with celery salt and garnish
with slices of cucumber.

— HARVEY WALLBANGER —

1 msr. vodka

1 msr. Galliano

orange juice

slice of orange

Pour vodka and Galliano into chilled
glass. Top with orange juice. Garnish
with slice of orange. Serve with a straw.

— SALTY DOG —

1½ msrs. vodka

ice cubes

grapefruit juice

salt and lemon juice to frost glass

wedge of lemon

Pour vodka over ice cubes in salt-frosted
glass. Fill with grapefruit juice. Garnish
with wedge of lemon.

— MOSCOW MULE —

2 msrs. vodka

1 msr. lemon juice

ice cubes

ginger beer

sprig of mint

Pour vodka and lemon juice over ice cubes in glass. Fill with ginger beer and stir to mix. Garnish with sprig of mint.

— WHITE RUSSIAN —

cubed and cracked ice

1 msr. vodka

1 msr. crème de caçao

1 msr. cream

grated nutmeg

Mix cracked ice with vodka, crème de caçao and cream in shaker. Strain over cubed ice in glass. Sprinkle with nutmeg.

— SCREWDRIVER —

1½ msrs. vodka

2 ice cubes

orange juice

1 maraschino cherry

slice of orange

Pour vodka over ice cubes in highball
glass. Fill with orange juice. Garnish
with cherry and slice of orange. Serve
with a straw.

— BLACK RUSSIAN —

3 msrs. vodka

1 msr. Kahlua

ice cubes

Pour vodka and Kahlua over ice-filled
glass.

— CHI CHI —

cracked ice

—

1½ msrs. vodka

—

1 msr. coconut cream

—

4 msrs. unsweetened pineapple juice

—

1 maraschino cherry

—

slice of pineapple

—

2 pineapple leaves

Place cracked ice in blender. Add vodka,
coconut cream and pineapple juice.
Blend for 10 seconds – any longer will
dilute drink. Strain into large glass.
Garnish with cherry, slice of pineapple
and leaves. Serve with a straw.

— BLUE LAGOON —

1 msr. vodka

—

1 msr. blue Curaçao

—

ice cubes

—

lemonade

—

3 cherries

Pour vodka and Curaçao into an ice-
filled goblet. Stir and fill with lemonade.
Decorate with cherries and serve with a
straw.

— BLOODY MARY —

¼ msr. lemon juice

—

2 drops Tabasco sauce

—

1 dash Worcestershire sauce

—

salt and pepper

—

2 msrs. vodka

—

ice cubes

—

tomato juice

—

stick of celery

—

celery salt and lemon juice to frost glass

Mix lemon juice, Tabasco sauce and
Worcestershire sauce in celery salt
frosted glass. Add salt and pepper to
taste. Add vodka and ice cubes. Top
with tomato juice and stir well. Serve
with stick of celery. (White rum, gin,
Tequila or akvavit can be substituted for
vodka.)

— FROZEN STRAWBERRY DAIQUIRI —

1½ msrs. light rum

—

½ msr. strawberry liqueur

—

juice of ½ lime

—

5 strawberries

—

crushed ice

—

1 maraschino cherry

Blend rum, liqueur, lime juice and 3 of
the strawberries with plenty of crushed
ice in blender until almost frozen. Pour
unstrained into a large goblet. Garnish
with remaining strawberries and cherry.
Serve with a short, thick straw.

BLUE HAWAIIAN

2 msrs. pineapple juice

1 msr. light rum

1 msr. blue Curaçao

1 msr. coconut cream

crushed ice

piece of pineapple

strip of coconut

1 cherry

2 pineapple leaves

Combine pineapple juice, rum, coconut cream and Curaçao with crushed ice in blender and mix well. Pour into glass and garnish with piece of pineapple, strip of coconut, cherry and leaves. Serve with a straw.

DAIQUIRI

3 msrs. light rum

1 msr. lemon or lime juice

1 teaspoon caster sugar

cracked ice

1½ slices of lemon or lime

Mix rum, lemon or lime juice and sugar with cracked ice in shaker. Strain into chilled glass. Add ½ slice of lemon or lime. Garnish with remaining slice of lemon or lime.

— MAI TAI —

crushed ice

2 msrs. light rum

1 msr. Jamaican rum

½ msr. Curaçao or other orange-
flavoured liqueur

½ msr. Orgeat or other almond-
flavoured syrup

½ msr. lemon or lime juice

sprig of mint

½ slice of pineapple

1 maraschino cherry

slice of kiwi fruit

Half-fill large goblet with ice. Mix in
light rum, Jamaican rum, Curaçao,
Orgeat and lemon or lime juice. Fill
glass with more crushed ice and stir
contents gently. Garnish with mint,
pineapple, cherry and kiwi fruit.

— ZOMBIE —

cracked ice

1 msr. dark rum

1 msr. Jamaican rum

1 msr. light rum

1 msr. lemon or lime juice

4 dashes passion fruit or orange juice

4 dashes apricot brandy

4 dashes cherry brandy

fresh fruit, such as pineapple, kiwi fruit,
papaya or paw paw, cherries, to garnish

Half fill blender with cracked ice. Add
dark rum, Jamaican rum, light rum,
lemon or lime juice, passion fruit or
orange juice, apricot brandy and cherry
brandy and blend well. Pour into large
glass. Garnish with fruit and serve with
straws.

— PLANTER'S PUNCH —

2 msrs. Jamaican rum

1 msr. lemon or lime juice

1 teaspoon Grenadine

1 dash Angostura bitters

ice cubes

soda water

1 hollowed-out pineapple, if desired

slice of orange

1 pineapple leaf

1 coloured cherry

Pour rum, lemon or lime juice,
Grenadine and bitters into mixing glass
half-filled with ice. Stir gently and pour
into hollowed-out pineapple, if desired,
or into large glass. Top with soda water.
Garnish with slice of orange, leaf and
coloured cherry.

— PINA COLADA —

cracked ice

1½ msrs. light rum

1 msr. pineapple juice

1 msr. coconut milk

½ msr. cream

1 maraschino cherry

piece of pineapple

1 hollowed-out coconut, if desired

Combine ice with rum, pineapple juice,
coconut milk and cream in shaker.
Shake until frosty. Strain into hollowed-
out coconut, if desired, or large glass.
Garnish with cherry and pineapple.
Serve with a straw.

— CUBA LIBRE —

1 msr. light rum

juice of ½ lime

ice cubes

cola

slice of lime

Pour rum and lime into an ice filled
highball glass and stir well. Fill with
cola. Garnish with slice of lime and
serve with a straw.

— BRANDY ALEXANDER —

cracked ice

⅓ msr. cream

⅓ msr. brandy

⅓ msr. crème de caçao

grated nutmeg

Mix ice with cream, brandy and crème
de caçao in shaker. Strain into glass.
Sprinkle with nutmeg.

— BETWEEN THE SHEETS —

cracked ice

¾ msr. rum

¾ msr. triple sec

¾ msr. brandy

juice of ½ lemon

twist of lemon or lime peel

Mix ice with rum, triple sec, brandy
and lemon juice in shaker. Strain into
Martini glass and garnish with twist of
lemon or lime peel.

— SIDECAR —

cracked ice

½ msr. brandy

¼ msr. Cointreau

¼ msr. lemon juice

Mix ice with brandy, Cointreau and
lemon juice in shaker. Strain into glass.

— STINGER —

cracked ice

⅔ msr. brandy

⅓ msr. white crème de menthe

Mix ice with brandy and crème de menthe in shaker. Strain into brandy glass or serve "on the rocks".

— B & B —

½ msr. Benedictine

½ msr. brandy

Pour Benedictine into liqueur glass. Carefully add brandy.

— SANGRIA —

2 tablespoons caster sugar

juice of 1 lemon

juice of 1 orange

1 orange, thinly sliced

1 lemon, thinly sliced

1 lime, thinly sliced

ice cubes

1 bottle red wine, chilled

Mix sugar, lemon and orange juice in a large pitcher until sugar has dissolved. Add sliced fruit, wine and plenty of ice and stir well. Serve in large wine glasses.

— KIR —

½ msr. crème de cassis

chilled dry white wine

Pour crème de cassis into tulip glass. Fill with white wine.

— MULLED WINE —

1 cup/8 msrs. water

1 stick cinnamon

6 cloves

6 allspice berries

1 bottle red wine

1 wine glass port

1 tablespoon sugar

peel from ½ lemon, cut into thin slices

slice of lemon

Combine water and spices in a saucepan and simmer for 20 minutes. Pour red wine into another large saucepan. Strain in the spiced water. Reserve spices for garnish. Add port and sugar and heat until mixture is almost boiling. Serve hot with thin slices of lemon peel and slice of lemon. Garnish with the spices, if desired.

— SUMMER WINE CUP —

selection of fresh fruit, such as strawberries, raspberries, peaches and blackcurrants

caster sugar

ice cubes

2 bottles chilled medium-dry white wine

2 msrs. Curaçao

1 msr. maraschino liqueur

2 hollowed-out pineapples, if desired

Place most of fruit in large punch bowl. Sprinkle with sugar. Add plenty of ice, then pour in wine, Curaçao and maraschino. Chill for 1 hour. Ladle in to glasses decorated with additional fruit or, if desired, serve in hollowed-out pineapples.

— MANGO BELLINI —

mango juice

chilled champagne

slice of mango

Fill champagne glass one-third full with
mango juice. Top with champagne. Stir
gently. Decorate with slice of mango.

— CHAMPAGNE COCKTAIL —

1 cube sugar

3 dashes Angostura bitters

½ msr. brandy

chilled champagne

piece of orange

1 maraschino cherry

Place sugar cube in champagne glass
and sprinkle with bitters. Add brandy.
Fill with champagne and stir gently.
Garnish with orange and cherry.

— RITZ FIZZ —

1 dash Amaretto

1 dash strained lemon juice

1 dash blue Curaçao

chilled champagne

1 rose petal, if desired

Mix Amaretto, lemon juice and
Curaçao in glass. Top with champagne.
Garnish with rose petal, if desired.

— BUCK'S FIZZ —

orange juice

1 dash Grenadine, if desired

chilled champagne

slice of lime

Fill glass one-third full with orange
juice. Add Grenadine. Top with
champagne. Garnish with slice of lime.

— GREEN DEMON —

1 msr. light rum

1 msr. melon liqueur

1 msr. vodka

cracked and cubed ice

lemonade

piece of watermelon

1 cherry

Combine rum, melon liqueur, vodka and cracked ice in shaker. Shake until frosty. Pour into large goblet over cubed ice. Fill with lemonade. Garnish with watermelon and cherry. Serve with straws.

— TEQUILA SUNRISE —

1 msr. Tequila

ice cubes

4 msrs. orange juice

2 dashes Grenadine

slice of orange

1 maraschino cherry

Pour Tequila over ice in glass. Stir in orange juice. Add Grenadine. Garnish with slice of orange and cherry. Serve with a straw.

— GOLD PASSION —

1 msr. passion fruit and white rum
spirit

1 msr. vodka

ice cubes

chilled pineapple juice

slice of pineapple

1 maraschino cherry

2 pineapple leaves

Pour passion fruit and white rum spirit
and vodka over ice cubes in large goblet.
Fill with pineapple juice and stir gently.
Garnish with slice of pineapple, cherry
and leaves. Serve with a straw.

— SINGAPORE SLING —

2 msrs. gin

1 msr. cherry brandy

1 msr. lemon juice

cracked and cubed ice

soda water

slice of lemon

slice of orange

1 maraschino cherry

sprig of mint

Combine gin, cherry brandy, lemon
juice and cracked ice in shaker and mix
well. Strain into large goblet or tall glass
over ice cubes. Fill with soda water.
Garnish with slices of lemon and
orange, cherry and mint.

51

— TROPICAL COCKTAIL —

1 msr. gin

1 msr. melon liqueur

2 msrs. tropical fruit juice

cracked ice

slices of melon, mango, kiwi fruit,
papaya or fruit of your choice

Combine gin, melon liqueur, fruit juice
and ice in shaker. Shake until frosty.
Pour into large goblet. Garnish with
fruit and serve with a straw.

— MELON SOUR —

1 msr. melon liqueur

2 msrs. lemon juice

1 egg white

cracked ice

2 melon balls

1 maraschino cherry

Combine melon liqueur, lemon juice,
egg white and ice in shaker. Shake until
frosty. Strain into glass. Garnish with
melon balls and cherry.

52

— KAHLUA CAFE DON JUAN —

lemon juice

brown sugar

¾ msr. dark rum

1 msr. Kahlua

hot coffee

cream

grated chocolate

Wipe the rim of large goblet with lemon juice and dip in brown sugar. Pour rum into goblet and ignite; twirling the flaming liquid for a few seconds. Add the Kahlua. Fill with coffee. Carefully pour cream over back of a teaspoon to float on top of drink. Sprinkle with chocolate.

— MARGARITA —

lemon juice and coarse salt for frosting

1½ msrs. Tequila

1 msr. lemon or lime juice

½ msr. triple sec or Cointreau

cracked ice

slice of lemon

wedge of lime

Wipe rim of glass with lemon juice and dip in salt to frost. Combine Tequila, triple sec or Cointreau, lemon or lime juice and ice in a shaker and mix well. Strain into glass and garnish with slice of lemon and wedge of lime.

— SILK STOCKINGS —

1½ msrs. Tequila

1 msr. white crème de caçao

1 dash Grenadine

1½ msrs. cream

crushed ice

ground cinnamon

1 maraschino cherry

Combine Tequila, crème de caçao, Grenadine and cream with ice in blender. Mix until frosty. Pour into glass. Sprinkle with cinnamon and garnish with cherry. Serve with straws.

— TEQUILA COCKTAIL —

cracked ice

2 msrs. Tequila

juice of ½ lemon

4 dashes Grenadine

1 dash egg white

slice of lemon

1 maraschino cherry

Combine ice with Tequila, lemon juice, Grenadine and egg white in shaker and mix well. Strain into glass. Garnish with slice of lemon and cherry.

— PIMMS —

1 msr. Pimms No.1

ice cubes

lemonade or ginger ale

slice of lemon

slice of orange

cucumber peel

sprig of mint

Pour Pimms over ice in large glass. Fill
with lemonade or ginger ale. Garnish
with slices of lemon and orange,
cucumber peel and mint.

— RUBY SHY —

1 msr. Malibu (coconut and white rum
spirit)

1 msr. blackcurrant cordial

ice cubes

lemonade

slice of coconut

grated coconut

Pour Malibu and blackcurrant cordial
over ice cubes in highball glass. Fill
with lemonade and stir well. Garnish
with coconut and serve with a straw.

— SHERRY FLIP —

cracked ice

2 msrs. sherry

1 teaspoon caster sugar

1 egg

grated nutmeg

Combine ice, sherry, sugar and egg in shaker and mix well. Strain into a wine glass. Sprinkle with nutmeg.

— HUMMER —

1 msr. Kahlua

1 msr. light rum

2 large scoops vanilla ice cream

grated chocolate

Combine Kahlua, rum and ice cream in blender and mix well. Pour into a glass. Sprinkle with chocolate.

— CREOLE COCKTAIL —

cracked and cubed ice

1 msr. Malibu (coconut and white rum spirit)

1 msr. orange juice

¾ msr. vodka

1 dash Grenadine

slice of orange

2 coloured cherries

2 slices of coconut

Combine cracked ice with Malibu, orange juice, vodka and Grenadine in shaker and mix well. Pour into large goblet with cubed ice. Garnish with slice of orange, cherries and slices of coconut.

— COFFEE BREAK —

cracked and cubed ice

1 msr. cold coffee

1 msr. Tia Maria

1 msr. milk

1 msr. Malibu (coconut and white rum spirit)

instant coffee powder or coffee beans, finely ground

3 slices of coconut

Combine ice, cold coffee, Tia Maria, milk and coconut liqueur in shaker and mix well. Strain and pour over cubed ice in large goblet. Sprinkle with instant or ground coffee. Garnish with slices of coconut.

— CAPUCINE —

cracked and crushed ice

1 msr. peppermint cordial

4 msrs. cream

grated chocolate

2 chocolate sticks

Combine cracked ice with peppermint
cordial and cream in shaker. Shake until
frosty. Strain into large wine glass. Add
crushed ice. Sprinkle with grated
chocolate and garnish with chocolate
sticks.

— MARMALADE —

1 msr. orange Curaçao

ice cubes

tonic water

kumquat or slice of orange

Pour Curaçao into an ice-filled glass.
Fill with tonic water and stir to mix.
Garnish with kumquat flower or slice of
orange.

── ROSY PIPPIN ──

1 dash Grenadine

1 dash lemon juice

¼ cup/4 msrs. apple juice

ginger ale

slice of apple

Add Grenadine and lemon juice to
apple juice and stir well. Pour into glass.
Fill with ginger ale. Garnish with slice
of apple.

── NURSERY FIZZ ──

orange juice

ginger ale

ice cubes

slice of orange

1 coloured cherry

Pour equal parts orange juice and ginger
ale over ice in large wine glass. Garnish
with orange and cherry. Serve with
straws.

— YOGURT FIZZ —

2 tablespoons yogurt

sparkling mineral water or soda water

salt

ice cubes

sprigs of mint

2 slices of cucumber

Mix yogurt and mineral or soda water in tall glass. Add salt and mint to taste. Add ice cubes and garnish with sprig of mint and cucumber.

— MICKEY MOUSE —

cola

ice cubes

1 scoop vanilla ice cream

whipped cream

2 maraschino cherries

Pour cola over ice in tall glass. Add ice cream. Top with whipped cream and garnish with cherries. Serve with straws and long-handled spoon.

— SHIRLEY TEMPLE —

ginger ale

ice cubes

2 dashes Grenadine

2 maraschino cherries

Pour ginger ale over ice in highball
glass. Stir in Grenadine. Garnish with
cherries.

— LEMONADE —

juice of 1 lemon

2 tablespoons sugar

cracked and cubed ice

water

spiral of lemon peel

slice of lemon

Pour lemon juice and sugar over cracked
ice in shaker. Mix well. Pour over cubed
ice into glass. Fill with water. Stir.
Garnish with spiral of lemon peel and
slice of lemon and serve with a straw.

— VIRGIN MARY —

4 msrs. tomato juice

½ msr. lemon juice

2 dashes Worcestershire sauce

1 dash Tabasco sauce

stick of cucumber

celery salt and lemon wedge to frost glass

Rub glass with lemon wedge and dip in celery salt to frost. Add tomato juice, lemon juice, Worcestershire sauce and Tabasco sauce and stir well. Serve with stick of cucumber.

— EGG NOGG —

cracked ice

1 egg

1 teaspoon caster sugar

10 msrs. milk

grated nutmeg or ground cinnamon

Combine ice, egg, sugar and milk in shaker. Mix well. Strain into goblet. Sprinkle with nutmeg or cinnamon.

GLOSSARY

ALMOND LIQUEUR   A liqueur flavoured with almonds and sweetened.

AMARETTO   An almond and apricot based liqueur, first made in Saronno, near Lake Como, Italy, during the 16th Century.

ANGOSTURA BITTERS   An infusion of aromatics from the West Indies, used very sparingly for flavouring cocktails and mixed drinks.

BENEDICTINE   A sweet, golden coloured, brandy based liqueur, flavoured with mixed herbs and originally made by Benedictine monks from Fécamp, Normandy, France.

BITTERS   An infusion of aromatics, usually prepared by blending aromatic or fruit substances with wine or spirit.

CAMPARI BITTERS   An Italian aperitif wine with strong, bitter taste and very red colour.

COINTREAU   A sweet, colourless liqueur flavoured with oranges and produced in Anjou, France.

CREME DE BANANE   A pungent, banana flavoured liqueur, which can be either white or straw coloured.

CREME DE CAÇAO   A very sweet, brandy based liqueur, made from Venezuelan cocoa beans. It has a cocoa-vanilla flavour and is chocolate brown in colour.

CREME DE CASSIS   A brandy based liqueur, flavoured with blackcurrants, originally from Dijon, France.

CREME DE MENTHE   A peppermint flavoured liqueur, based on grain spirit, which can be green, white or pink.

CURAÇAO   A sweet liqueur, which can be blue, white or orange, and which is made with peel of oranges, originally from Curaçao in the West Indies.

DRAMBUIE   A Scotch whisky based liqueur, flavoured with herbs and heather honey.

FRAISE LIQUEUR   A liqueur flavoured with strawberries.

GALLIANO   A golden coloured liqueur, flavoured with liquorice and aniseed, produced in Milan, Italy.

GRENADINE   A red, non-alcoholic, French fruit syrup made from pomegranates, and possessing a slight redcurrant flavour.

KAHLUA   A rich brown liqueur made from Mexican coffee beans.

KUMMEL   A liqueur flavoured with caraway.

MALIBU   A coconut and light Jamaican rum spirit. Used in several exotic cocktails.

MARASCHINO   A colourless liqueur from Italy made with sour maraschino cherries and their crushed kernels.

MELON LIQUEUR   A light, fragrant, melon flavoured, green coloured liqueur, served in a variety of new cocktail recipes.

PASSION FRUIT AND WHITE RUM SPIRIT   A sweet fragrant liquid made from white rum spirit, flavoured with passion fruit.

PORT   A full bodied wine, fortified with brandy during fermentation, which comes from the Duoro Valley in the north of Portugal.

SHERRY   A wine fortified with brandy, which is added after fermentation. Originally from Spain, it now also comes from Australia, South Africa and Cyprus.

SUGAR SYRUP   A mixture of equal parts sugar and water boiled just until sugar is dissolved.

TEQUILA   A clear spirit distilled in Mexico from a species of agave plant, similar to cactus.

TIA MARIA   A Jamaican rum based liqueur flavoured with coffee and spices.

TRIPLE SEC   A colourless Curaçao, flavoured with orange peel, and sweetened.

INDEX

Almond Liqueur, 63
Amaretto, 63
Anchovy Toasties, 22
Angostura Bitters, 63
Avocado Dip, 20

B & B, 45
Bellini, Mango, 48
Benedictine, 63
Between the Sheets, 44
Bikini, 34
Bitters, 63
Bitters, Angostura, 63
Bitters, Campari, 63
Black Russian, 37
Bloodshot, 34
Bloody Mary, 39
Blue Hawaiian, 40
Blue Lagoon, 38
Bourbon Mint Julep, 29
Brandy Alexander, 43
Bronx Cocktail, 28
Buck's Fizz, 49
Bullshot, 33

Campari Bitters, 63
Capucine, 58
Champagne Cocktail, 48
Cheesy Puffs, 21
Chi Chi, 38
Coffee Break, 57
Cointreau, 63
Crème de Banane, 63
Crème de Caçao, 63
Crème de Cassis, 63
Crème de Menthe, 63
Creole Cocktail, 57
Cuba Libre, 43
Curacáo, 63

Daiquiri, 40
Daiquiri, Frozen Strawberry, 39
Drambuie, 63
Dry Manhattan, 30
Dry Martini, 24

Egg Nogg, 62

Fraise Liqueur, 63
Frozen Strawberry Daiquiri, 39

Galliano, 63
Gin, Pink, 25
Gold Passion, 51
Green Demon, 50
Grenadine, 63

Harvey Wallbanger, 35
Hot Spicy Sauce, 20
Hummer, 56

John (or Tom) Collins, 28

Kahlua, 63
Kahlua Cafe Don Juan, 53
Kir, 46
Kummel, 63

Lemonade, 61

Mai Tai, 41
Malibu, 63
Mango Bellini, 48
Manhattan (dry), 30
Manhattan (sweet), 30
Maraschino, 63
Margarita, 53
Marmalade, 58
Martini (dry), 24
Martini (sweet), 24
Melon Liqueur, 63
Melon Sour, 52
Mickey Mouse, 60
Mint Julep, Bourbon, 29
Moscow Mule, 36
Mulled Wine, 47

Negroni, 26
Nursery Fizz, 59

Old Fashioned, 31

Passion Fruit & White Rum Spirit, 63
Peppers with Creamy Cucumber Dip, 21
Pimms, 55
Pina Colada, 42
Pink Gin, 25
Pink Lady, 23
Plantain Chips, 20
Planter's Punch, 42
Port, 63

Ramoz Fizz, 27
Ritz Fizz, 49
Rob Roy, 32
Roles Royce, 26
Rosy Pippin, 59
Ruby Shy, 55
Rusty Nail, 31

Salty Dog, 35
Sangria, 46
Screwdriver, 37
Sherry, 63
Sherry Flip, 56
Shirley Temple, 61
Sidecar, 44
Silk Stockings, 54
Silver Streak, 25
Singapore Sling, 51
Spicy Nuts, 22
Stinger, 45
Strawberry Daiquiri, Frozen, 39
Strawberry Dawn, 27
Sugar Syrup, 63
Summer Wine Cup, 47
Surf Rider, 33
Sweet Manhattan, 30
Sweet Martini, 24

Tequila, 63
Tequila Cocktail, 54
Tequila Sunrise, 50
Tia Maria, 63
Tom (or John) Collins, 28
Triple Sec, 63
Tropical Cocktail, 52

Virgin Mary, 62

Wallbanger, Harvey, 35
Whisky Cobbler, 29
Whisky Sour, 32
White Lady, 23
White Russian, 36
Wine Cup, Summer, 47
Wine, Mulled, 47

Yogurt Fizz, 60

Zombie, 41